Nancy Oloro

The Dancing Suitcase

J·A·W·S

Illustrated by
Tony Morris

Series Editor: Karen Morrison

Heinemann

About the Author

Nancy Oloro was born and grew up in Uganda. She studied literature and performing arts before going to Zambia, where she still lives. She now teaches literature and English language, and writes plays and poems as well as children's stories.

Heinemann Educational Publishers
Halley Court, Jordan Hill, Oxford OX2 8EJ
A division of Reed Educational & Professional Publishing Ltd

Heinemann Educational Books (Nigeria) Ltd
PMB 5205, Ibadan
Heinemann Educational Botswana Publishers (Pty) Ltd
PO Box 10103, Village Post Office, Gaborone, Botswana

FLORENCE PRAGUE MADRID ATHENS
MELBOURNE AUCKLAND TOKYO SINGAPORE KUALA LUMPUR
PORTSMOUTH NH (USA) MEXICO CITY CHICAGO
SAO PAULO JOHANNESBURG KAMPALA NAIROBI

British Library Cataloguing in Publication Data
A catalogue record for this book is available
from the British Library

ISBN 0 435 89249 5

Glossary
Difficult words are listed alphabetically on pages 58–9

Edited by Christine King
Designed by The Point
Printed and bound in Great Britain by Cox & Wyman Ltd, Reading, Berkshire

96 97 98 99 10 9 8 7 6 5 4 3 2 1

CONTENTS

CHAPTER ONE

The villagers of Kareu tell stories about a girl called Lilai. She was very beautiful. When she passed by, all heads turned to look at her. Everyone she met fell under the spell of her beauty.

Lilai was an orphan. Her parents died when she was very young, so she had hardly known them. She lived with her Aunt Asio's family. Her cousin, Ationo, was the same age as Lilai. Aunt Asio loved both girls equally and she and her husband always treated them the same way.

But Ationo never truly accepted her cousin as a sister. Ationo was an only child, and she was used to being treated specially. When Lilai came to live with them, Ationo found it difficult to share her parents' affection and attention. She began to think of Lilai as a rival and an enemy. She always found ways of reminding her cousin that she did not really belong to their family.

Ationo tried to get Lilai into trouble by telling lies about her. She hoped her parents would begin to dislike Lilai. But she did not succeed. Lilai was a cheerful child who grew up to be kind and responsible. She was as good as she was beautiful.

Everyone loved her, and no matter how Ationo tried, she couldn't change that.

One day, Aunt Asio received a message that her mother was very sick.

'Grandmother needs someone to look after her,' Aunt Asio told Lilai, a worried look on her face. 'I wish I could go myself, but I'm needed at home.'

'Then I will go and help her!' said Lilai at once. She loved her grandmother, and she was pleased to have a chance of helping the old woman who was always kind to her.

'Are you sure?' her aunt asked. 'It's quite a long way to go, you know.'

'Of course I'm sure,' said Lilai firmly. 'I'll start getting ready right now.'

Ationo had been listening to her mother and her cousin. In her mind she sneered at Lilai. Imagine volunteering for a lot of hard work!

Lilai was very excited as she packed for her trip. But, although she would not worry her aunt by telling her, deep down Lilai did have some fears about the journey. In order to reach her grandmother's house, she had to walk a very long

'Then I will go and help her!' said Lilai at once.

way, passing through forests and swamps. The journey could only be done in one day if she walked very, very quickly. If not, she would have to spend the night sleeping in the forest. To calm her fears, Lilai told herself that she would easily make the trip in one day.

The next day Lilai started her journey at sunrise. She packed her own belongings together with the presents that Aunt Asio was sending to Grandmother. It was quite a load. But Lilai was excited to be off and didn't dream of complaining. She picked up the bundle and set off on her adventure.

She decided that she would walk quickly and jog or run when she could to make sure that she made it to her grandmother's in one day. As she hurried along, she sang any song that came into her head. The more songs she sang, the faster she went.

By twelve o'clock Lilai felt very tired. She found a huge shady tree to rest under and settled down on the cool ground. She closed her eyes and allowed her body to relax. She decided to rest for only fifteen minutes then carry on. But Lilai was very tired, and within a few minutes she was fast asleep.

CHAPTER TWO

Lilai was woken up by a loud thud on the ground.
She jumped up in fright and for a few seconds she
didn't know where she was. She rubbed the sleep
out of her eyes so that she could focus, and
suddenly it dawned on her. She was furious with
herself for being such a fool. How could she fall
asleep and waste precious time? She looked around
for her bundle so that she could move on.

But, to her surprise, an old woman was watching
her. At her feet, the woman had a bundle that
looked twice as heavy as Lilai's. The old woman had
her eyes fixed steadfastly on Lilai but she remained
silent.

Somebody had to say something! Lilai tried to
speak, but to her dismay no sound came out of her
mouth. She stood there staring back at the old
woman with her mouth open. The woman did not
react at all. She just continued watching Lilai with a
strange expression on her face.

Suddenly Lilai realised that the strange
expression was one of pain. The woman's heavy
bundle was not lying on the ground! It was actually
lying firmly on her feet, which were now quite

squashed. This made Lilai spring into action.

'Forgive me!' Lilai said. 'I didn't see that your bundle was actually lying on your feet. Here I am stupidly staring at you instead of helping you.'

As she spoke, Lilai hauled the heavy bundle off the old woman's feet.

'Thank you so much, my child,' the old woman said in a weak voice. 'If it wasn't for you, I don't know what I would have done!'

'You're welcome,' replied Lilai. 'I'm just happy that I could help.'

'I'm sorry I disturbed your sleep,' continued the old woman. 'I was trying to put this back on my head, but I struggled and it fell down and landed on my feet. Somehow, I felt too weak to pull myself free. Lucky for me, the noise the bundle made woke you up!'

Lilai and the old woman chatted on and got acquainted. The old woman's name was Atai. They soon discovered that they were headed in the same direction and they were both pleased to have some company.

Before they set out together, Lilai insisted that Atai take her lighter load. She would carry the old woman's bundle. Atai was reluctant. She felt it was unfair for Lilai to take the heavy load. But Lilai was determined. She picked up the woman's bundle and gave her the lighter one.

'Come on, let's move,' she said.

As they moved out of the trees, Lilai realised that she had slept for far too long. The sun was already starting to go down. She would have to speed up or sleep in the forest.

Lilai walked a bit faster, but Atai soon fell behind. Lilai stopped and waited. The old woman noticed Lilai's impatience and she offered to take back her bundle so that Lilai could move on. Lilai refused. She could not leave the old woman behind, even if it meant she would have to sleep in the forest. At least she would not be alone.

For a while, they walked on without talking. Both Lilai and Atai were lost in their own worlds. Lilai was thinking about the long night ahead in the forest. She did not take any notice of her companion until Atai asked, 'Where are you actually going?'

Lilai came out of her thoughts and explained about her grandmother. She told Atai that she still had quite a way to go and that she was worried about sleeping in the forest.

She picked up the woman's bundle and gave her the lighter one.

8

Atai smiled. 'You shall not sleep in the forest, my child. I am heading home, and my home is not far from your path. You must spend the night with me.'

Lilai could not believe her luck. As the fear of not knowing where she would spend the night vanished, the load she was carrying seemed lighter. Lilai smiled and offered thanks to her ancestors. They were certainly wide awake and looking after her!

She and Atai chatted non-stop as they went along. They talked so much that they didn't notice the distance. After a few hours, they came to a crossroads where the road split into three different routes. They took the left-hand path to Atai's home, and after about half an hour they arrived.

Atai prepared a tasty meal for Lilai, and wouldn't let the girl help her.

'No, my dear,' she insisted. 'If it wasn't for you, I would have had a very hard journey. The least I can do is look after you now.'

So Lilai enjoyed her meal. Then, tired out after all her travelling, she slept peacefully through the night.

Atai woke Lilai early next morning, and gave her a good breakfast.

'Now remember, you can stay the night here again on your way back,' said Atai.

'I will,' promised Lilai. 'Thank you!'

She set off for her grandmother's home, running most of the way.

CHAPTER THREE

As soon as Lilai saw her grandmother, tears rushed
into her eyes. Just by looking at her grandmother's
long thin face, tight with pain, she knew that all was
not well. She felt very bad that her journey had
taken an extra day. Lilai held her grandmother
tightly for a while and then she started to work.

First, Lilai made a fire and warmed some water
for her grandmother to use for bathing. To her
shock, the old woman could not even get up from
her bed without help. Lilai helped her up and left
her to wash. While Grandmother was washing, Lilai
changed the bedding and put clean fresh sheets on
the bed. She used the ones that her grandmother
always kept ready for visitors. Then she helped her
grandmother back to bed and tucked her in. She
left her while she made a bowl of sweet millet
porridge. Finally, when her grandmother was sound
asleep, Lilai set about cleaning the whole house.
She sang as she worked.

With Lilai there, Grandmother soon felt better.
Very gradually, her strength and cheerfulness
returned to her. The doctor visited and said that
her health was greatly improved.

'It seems like your granddaughter is good medicine!' he said, smiling.

'The best there is,' said Grandmother.

Lilai just smiled.

Lilai helped her grandmother for two weeks. After that, it was clear that she was well enough to manage on her own. Lilai began to talk about going home. Grandmother tried to persuade her to stay, but Lilai was missing her aunt and uncle. She even missed her unkind cousin Ationo, although she knew Ationo would not feel the same way.

So, on Sunday morning, Lilai kissed her grandmother and set out on the long journey home.

This journey was much harder than the first one. Lilai's bundle was heavy with presents for the family. In addition, it had rained heavily and the swamps and rivers had risen quite a bit. Lilai had to wade through cold water several times. She tried to move slowly and carefully, but it was no use. The mud and water sucked at her feet and she kept falling over. Each time she fell she had to clean the mud and water from her face and arms. Even the paths were muddy and slippery, and Lilai had to move very slowly. The presents in her bundle

The mud and water sucked at her feet.

weighed her down and she wished she could throw them all in the swamp.

It was dusk by the time she reached the crossroads. She thought gratefully about Atai's invitation to spend the night with her. The thought of a nice warm bed and a good meal cheered Lilai up. She realised that she was really tired and hungry.

She took the path to the old woman's home. Soon she saw the hut in the distance. The sight of it made her walk much faster than before and it didn't take long for her to reach the front door.

Lilai knocked softly and said, 'Hello, it's me, Lilai.'

A frail, feeble voice answered and asked her to come in. Lilai was surprised. It did not sound like the old woman she had got to know. She wondered whether she was at the wrong hut, but as she pushed the door open, she recognised the furniture. This was definitely the right place! As she stepped into the room, a weak voice exclaimed from the darkness, 'It's you, my daughter. I'm so glad that you're here.'

CHAPTER FOUR

Lilai quickly put her heavy bundle down on the floor. She knew immediately that something was wrong.

It was very dark inside the hut and Lilai struggled to focus her eyes. As her vision adjusted to the light, she saw that her friend was lying in bed. Atai looked like she had been sick for a long time. When she saw Lilai, the old woman tried to smile, but her face was filled with pain and she started to cough. Lilai rushed over to her bed and knelt down next to her.

'What is wrong, Mama?' Lilai asked softly.

The old woman explained that she had suddenly felt ill and that she could not find help. Her nearest neighbour was away, and no one else had come past the hut. 'But,' she explained, 'I held on. I knew that you would come back this way. I prayed that your grandmother was better and that you would come soon. And now my prayers have been answered.'

Atai finished speaking with another bout of coughing. Lilai put her hand on her thin arm.

'Don't worry any more. I am here,' she said.

'What is wrong, Mama?' Lilai asked softly.

Lilai lit the lamp and looked around. It was clear that the old woman had not been able to do anything for herself. It was also likely that she had not eaten anything for a while.

Lilai set to work. She quickly cleaned the house and lit the other lamps. She fetched wood from outside the door and soon had a fire burning. The house already felt better – it was warm and light and clean. The old woman said nothing. She just dozed and coughed from time to time.

Lilai found some fairly fresh sweet potatoes in a corner near the fire. She put them on to cook. While they were cooking she found some blankets to make herself a bed. When the food was ready, she fed Atai.

'Thank you, you are an angel,' said the old woman, before she dozed off again.

Lilai blew out the lamps and went to bed. She was so exhausted that she fell asleep as soon as she wrapped the blankets around herself.

The next morning, Lilai was up early. She looked around the compound. There were a few clay pots lying close to a well-worn path. Lilai guessed that this was where the old woman fetched water. Her guess was correct and soon she had all the pots filled with clear fresh water. She lit the fire and soon had some water boiling for Atai's bath.

Lilai's movements woke the old woman. At first she was confused, then suddenly she remembered that Lilai had arrived in the night. She found it hard to believe that the girl was so kind and helpful. Here she was, treating her as if she was one of her own blood relatives!

Lilai saw that her friend was awake. 'How are you feeling, Mama?' she asked. 'Well enough to have a bath? It will make you feel better.'

While the old woman bathed behind her hut, Lilai changed the bedding and washed the blankets. When Atai had finished bathing, Lilai asked what she wanted for her morning meal. Lilai's help and kindness made the old woman feel much better. She smiled and told Lilai what she wanted.

After they had eaten, the old woman showed Lilai her granary. The granary had sacks of millet in it. Then the woman asked Lilai to take half of the millet and thresh it. Lilai thought this was a strange request, but she did as she was asked. It took her about two hours to finish the job. She went back to the old woman to find out what to do with the millet.

Atai asked Lilai to divide the millet into two portions and grind one portion into flour.

Grinding the millet with a stone was difficult, but Lilai did not complain. She worked happily and kept herself going by singing.

When she had finished grinding the millet, the old woman told her to use half of the finely ground flour to make millet bread. She was to keep the other half to use later on. The woman also showed Lilai where she kept her smoked meat. Again she asked Lilai to use half of the meat and prepare it so they could eat it with the millet bread. Lilai did as she was asked but she wondered why the old woman wanted half of everything.

'What could she be saving it for?' she asked herself. 'Could she be saving it for the spirits?'

The thought made her shiver, so she just got on with what the old woman had asked her to do.

When the food was cooked, she called Atai, who again instructed her to serve half and leave half. Lilai did exactly this. She took the food to the old woman and they ate together. When they finished eating, it was already late in the afternoon. Lilai turned to the old woman and said that she was going to leave for home.

'No! You can't go now,' protested Atai. 'It is already too late. You shall go tomorrow.'

Lilai realised that the old woman was right and agreed to stay for another night.

The next day, it was Atai who got up early. She was feeling much better. She wanted to prepare a present for Lilai, but she did not want Lilai to see what she was doing.

When Lilai woke up, she found Atai sitting outside the hut with a battered old suitcase next to her. Lilai wondered whether the old woman wanted to leave with her.

Instead, the woman gave the suitcase to Lilai and said, 'There is a present for you inside the suitcase, my child. I wanted to thank you for your kindness and concern.'

Lilai was very surprised. She took the case and the old woman continued, 'There are, however, two conditions. First, you must under no circumstances open the case until you get home. Second, please bring it back to me when you next go to your grandmother's.'

Atai smiled. 'It is a very old suitcase, and it is very special.'

Lilai could see nothing special about the suitcase,

but she happily agreed. Then she picked up her belongings and bid her friend farewell. Soon she was on her way home, running and singing all the way.

CHAPTER FIVE

The sun was going down by the time Lilai reached her village. The young girls of her age were fetching water for their families and a few lazy ones were half-heartedly looking for twigs to start the fires for cooking the evening meal. When the girls saw Lilai coming, they all ran up to her excitedly. Her friends embraced her and the whole group escorted her home. They had really missed her.

At home, her aunt and uncle were delighted to see her back. Even Ationo was happy to see her cousin back, because she knew her grandmother would have sent her a gift.

Everyone bombarded Lilai with questions.

'How is Grandmother?'

'How was the trip?'

'Did you meet anyone on the way?'

'Are you well?'

And finally from Ationo, 'What did you bring for me?'

Lilai answered most of the questions and then she started unpacking and distributing the gifts that she had brought for each one of them. Finally only the suitcase was left. It was neatly tied up and it drew everyone's attention. Ationo could not hold her curiosity in any longer. She demanded, rather than asked, what it was.

Lilai began to explain. She told them about the old woman and her illness and how she had helped her to feel better.

'Yes, yes,' said Ationo impatiently, 'that's all very well, but come on, open your gift. I want to see what the old woman gave you.'

Lilai took a deep breath and wiped her hands on her sides. She did not know what to expect. Everyone else was as anxious as Lilai to see what was inside the case.

'OK, I'll open it now,' said Lilai as she spread a papyrus mat on the floor. She put her suitcase down on it and started untying the string around it. Ationo was very impatient with Lilai's speed. She stepped forward and declared, 'You are too slow. Here, let me do it for you.'

'No!' Lilai stopped her. 'I will do it myself!'

Ationo had no choice but to wait. She sat still and silent, but in her heart she hoped that the gift would turn out to be a trivial, scruffy thing.

Finally, all the string was undone and Lilai slowly peeled away the paper that had been used to wrap the gift. Paper after paper fell off on to the floor without revealing the contents. Lilai wondered when the old woman had done all this. Then suddenly, there it was!

It was simply magnificent. Lilai and her family stared at the contents of the package. They were all speechless. No one had ever seen anything like this before!

The old woman had given Lilai a red velvet dress, red shoes and a lovely red handbag to match. But that was not all! On top of the dress there were a necklace and bracelet of ruby red precious stones. It was the glowing brightness of the jewels which held everyone's attention. They knew immediately that the jewels were real and valuable.

Lilai could not contain herself. She touched her gifts. Tears filled her eyes and rolled down her beautiful face. This was like a dream come true, and Lilai was lost in her thoughts. However, she was soon jolted back to reality by Ationo who said rudely, 'So, try them on. If the clothes don't fit you, at least they'll fit me!'

Ationo sounded faint and far away to Lilai. However, Lilai realised that her cousin's voice was

It was simply magnificent.

bitter with jealousy. She was wondering what to do when Aunt Asio found her voice and said softly, 'Lilai my daughter, you are very lucky. In all my life and with all the grey hairs that I have on my head, I have never seen such things happening! Why don't you go and try on your gifts? Let us see how you look in them. I am very certain that each and every thing is going to fit you perfectly. The old woman must have appreciated your help a great deal.'

Lilai picked up her gift and walked into her room. When she finally came out it seemed as though the old woman had taken her measurements. The dress and the shoes fitted perfectly. And the jewellery was magnificent! The bracelet neatly fitted Lilai's slim wrist, while the necklace glowed like burning crimson coals around her neck. She looked like a queen. Ationo thought she would burst with jealousy and she began to make a plan.

Lilai's gift changed Ationo. She suddenly became very friendly and helpful to everyone. Aunt Asio wondered what had come over her daughter. However, she was very happy with the new Ationo. Lilai also wondered about her cousin. This behaviour was not natural in Ationo, and Lilai wondered what she was after. She did not have to wait long to find out!

A few weeks later, a message arrived from Grandmother. It said that she was going away on a visit to her other daughter and needed Lilai to take care of her home while she was away. There were many things that she could not leave unattended. When Ationo heard this message she was furious. Inwardly, she believed that Grandmother had given Lilai the wondrous gifts. She thought that Lilai had lied about the old woman because she did not want Ationo to know where the gift came from. Ationo called her grandmother some rude names, and then she made up her mind. Lilai would not go! She, Ationo, would go and look after the household and collect her reward.

'It's not fair!' she complained. 'Lilai saw Grandmother last time. I haven't seen her for two years. Why is she going? It's not fair! I never get a chance to do anything.'

Both her parents looked at each other. They did not know what to say. Ationo had never volunteered to help anyone before in her life. Finally, it was Lilai who spoke.

'Ationo can go if she likes. I have missed quite a

bit of school work, and of course she is right, I did
see Grandmother recently.'

Ationo smiled a sly smile. 'Can I go, Mother?
Please let me!'

Aunt Asio looked at the girls. She wished Lilai
was not so fair and that Ationo was not so mean.
But eventually, she had to agree. Ationo would go
and look after her grandmother's place.

CHAPTER SIX

Ationo was very excited about her trip. When she closed her eyes, she could imagine the wonderful gifts she would receive from her grandmother.

Aunt Asio made preparations for Ationo's journey. She packed food and presents for her grandmother and sister into a bundle for Ationo to carry.

But Ationo looked at the bundle and said, 'You must be joking! Do you expect me to carry that heavy thing all the way? I am not a donkey!'

Aunt Asio was very angry with her daughter. She raised her voice and said, 'You are not supposed to be going on this trip at all. It is your own greed that you wish to satisfy. Now, either you take these gifts along with you, or you don't go at all!'

Ationo glared at her mother. She did not want to carry the bundle, but she didn't want to let Lilai go and get more presents.

'And don't forget Atai's suitcase,' said Lilai. 'She said she would like it back the next time I visited Grandmother, so you may as well take it.'

This made Ationo sulk even more, but she remembered the good things that had been packed

Aunt Asio was very angry with her daughter.

in the suitcase, and picked it up. She picked up the bundle with her other hand.

'Now, be careful,' said her mother. 'Some of the gifts are breakable.'

Ationo said nothing. Not even goodbye! She just took the luggage and started out on her journey.

She walked quickly and silently along the narrow road. After a short while she felt tired and decided to rest. She remembered her mother's warnings about the breakable presents, but she did not care. So she dumped the bundle and suitcase roughly on the ground and sat on them. She took out some juice and drank it all.

Ationo rested for a time, then she set off again. When the sun was overhead, she decided that it was time for her midday meal. Ationo again dumped her burdens down on the ground and sat on them. She took out her food and was about to start eating it when an old man came by. He looked very frail and old and he used a walking stick to support his failing strength. He carried a small bundle in his other hand. As he sat down, he cheerfully waved at the girl. Then he sighed deeply and put his head between his folded knees.

Ationo completely ignored the old man and

started eating her food. When she was half way through her food, the old man suddenly lifted up his head, cleared his throat and said, 'My daughter, don't you have pity on an old man like me? I have been walking for days on this endless journey. I ran out of food a few days ago. I still have a long way to go. Please will you spare me some of your own food?'

Ationo looked at him. 'How was I to know that you didn't have any food? You should have said something when you sat down,' she retorted.

'My daughter,' replied the old man, 'I hoped you would offer without me having to ask. You know that is part of our culture, our African culture. Our elders taught us that whenever you meet a stranger, you should offer him or her what you are eating. They also taught us not to ask for food if someone is eating. We were taught to wait patiently until we are offered any. I hoped that you would behave as you should.'

'Sorry, old man, the culture you are talking about died and was buried with the likes of you,' Ationo retorted ungraciously. 'We are now living in a different world, a new world, with mixed cultures. I think everyone should sort out their own problems.

These are modern times, and we are modern people. Anyway, you can have these leftovers, I was about to throw them away anyway.'

Instead of reacting to her rudeness, the old man answered, 'Thank you, my daughter, may our ancestors bless you.'

He took the food that Ationo offered.

'Hurry up with my container,' ordered Ationo. 'I have a long way to go and I have to get moving.'

'Where are you going to?' asked the old man.

'I'm going along this road, I may go as far as Tididiek,' Ationo snapped impatiently, wishing he would hurry.

'Oh!' exclaimed the old man. 'That's good. I'm going that way too. At least I will now have some company.'

Ationo rolled her eyes. She didn't want the old man for company. She began to wonder how she could get rid of him. She watched the old man who was trying to remove the fishbones that she had thrown among the bread. Eventually, after trying for a while, he gave up and sadly gave Ationo back her container.

'I thought you were hungry!' she said sarcastically. 'But it seems you were not.'

The old man said nothing. He simply stood up and brushed the leaves off his clothes. He bent and picked up his walking stick and his bundle. Soon he was tottering along the winding path. Ationo watched the diminishing figure. The old man looked just like a bundle of rags moving along the path.

She followed the old man's footprints and soon caught up with him. For a short while she pretended to walk alongside him, but then she said, 'Is that how you are going to walk? Can't you go any faster? You are like a tortoise!'

'My daughter,' replied the old man sadly, 'one day you will be in my shoes. Maybe then you will be more understanding and patient.'

'Your age is just an excuse,' said Ationo unkindly. 'I'm sure even when you were a young man you were always very slow!' She continued, 'In any case, if you are going to be so slow, then goodbye. I have to hurry up.'

The old man again said nothing. Ationo found herself feeling silly when the old man did not say anything. Inside her head she had a nagging thought of Lilai's jewels. Maybe Lilai had told the truth about the old woman. Maybe this old man

'Your age is just an excuse,' said Ationo unkindly.

could afford to give her something worth showing off. She was still deciding what to do when the old man said, 'You could help me by carrying my luggage. That may help me go faster.'

Ationo quickly agreed. She remembered that Lilai had carried the old woman's luggage. But, after they had walked for a short distance, Ationo became impatient. The old man's speed had hardly changed. She tried to be patient and think of the jewels but finally she could not.

'You made me carry your luggage so that you could walk faster. But it looks like you are even slower than before!' she declared.

After this declaration, Ationo walked faster, leaving the old man behind. For a while she played a cruel game. She walked for a while and then waited for the old man. When he had almost caught up, she moved on again taking his luggage with her. This did not give the old man any chance to rest, and he struggled after the awful girl.

However, Ationo soon got tired of the game. She sat down and waited in the shade. When the old man reached her he was exhausted.

'Here's your luggage back, old man. I am moving on,' she said.

'Please can I have some water before you leave?' asked the old man.

Ationo just laughed her mean laugh and said, 'Surely you don't expect me to carry your water as well as your luggage! There's a stream down there – go and have a drink. I am going on.'

The old man just sighed and watched her as she walked away.

CHAPTER SEVEN

Ationo hurried on along the footpath till she came to the spot where the roads crossed. She remembered Lilai's directions and soon she was on her way towards the old woman's home. It did not take her long to find it.

When Atai heard that she was Lilai's cousin, she treated her like an old friend.

She prepared a tasty meal for Ationo. While she was cooking, she said, 'How kind of you to return my suitcase. As I told your cousin, it is a very special suitcase.'

Ationo looked at the battered old case on the floor and thought, 'A special suitcase? How can a suitcase be special? It's what's in it that matters – and there'd better be something good in it for me!'

But she didn't say anything. She just ate her good meal and fell fast asleep in the comfortable bed that Atai prepared for her.

Very early the next day, Atai woke Ationo up and offered her some more food. Ationo ate well, and she did remember to thank the old woman before she left for her grandmother's home. As she walked, she smiled to herself. Everything seemed to

'It is a very special suitcase.'

be going according to plan. She felt so good that she started to sing. She was still singing when she reached her grandmother's.

Grandmother was surprised to see Ationo instead of Lilai. But she decided to welcome her other grandchild in the same way. Soon a hearty meal was on the fire. While it cooked, Ationo was offered a warm bath filled with herbs to soothe her tired muscles. Ationo enjoyed the attention, but she could not help thinking that her grandmother had prepared all these nice things for Lilai.

After the meal Ationo pretended to be very tired and went off to have a nap. She knew that her grandmother wanted to unwrap the bundle of gifts that she had carried, and she spitefully decided to delay.

When Ationo woke up, she fetched her bundle and invited her grandmother to open it. As Grandmother unwrapped the parcels, her smile dropped from her face. The clay pots were broken. The fresh eggs were broken. The dried fish lay mangled and mashed up in the groundnut paste. It was a horrible sight. Ationo just shrugged her shoulders and said, 'My mother must have packed carelessly. Sorry!'

Grandmother said nothing. She was too upset to speak.

Before Grandmother left to visit her other daughter, she tried to teach Ationo the chores that she was to perform. But it was no use! Grandmother no longer trusted Ationo and she worried that Ationo would not do anything properly once she left. She wondered often why Asio had sent Ationo instead of Lilai.

Ationo on the other hand could not wait for her grandmother to leave.

'How long will you be gone?' she asked.

'Well,' replied Grandmother. 'I'm not sure. It all depends on your aunt.'

'Don't expect me to stay here for ever!' moaned Ationo. 'I have to get back home as soon as I can.'

This was the final straw for Grandmother.

'Ationo, I did not ask you to come here. I asked for Lilai. Why did you come if you knew that you did not want to stay here? You can go back,' shouted Grandmother angrily.

'OK, I will!' shouted Ationo, who by now was just as angry. 'I will go back tomorrow. I want nothing to do with a mean old woman like you!'

Grandmother felt very unhappy. She could not

believe that this awful child was her grandchild. All the others were kind and helpful. It was only Ationo who was mean and spiteful. She felt glad that Ationo had decided to leave – she was sure that her household would have been neglected under her anyway.

Ationo was also relieved that she could leave. She decided that she would rush back to the old woman and try to get a present out of her as soon as possible.

She woke up very early the next day and gathered her belongings. She refused to even bid her grandmother farewell. As she walked away, she heard her grandmother mutter, 'Go well, my mean daughter, and give my regards to your family.'

Ationo's heart was beating very fast and she could not stop the smile that kept playing on her lips. Her greedy little feet carried her much faster than usual and she reached the crossroads faster than she expected. She quickly made her way to the old woman's home.

As she reached the hut, Ationo stopped. She could not believe her eyes.

Oh no! she thought. Not him, please, not him!

But there, sitting in the entrance to the old

woman's hut, was the old man that Ationo had taunted earlier. He was sitting with his head between his knees again. His walking stick lay on the ground. Ationo felt a shiver down her spine. She hoped he had not talked to the old woman about her.

She walked towards the hut slowly. The old man heard her footsteps and looked up. When he saw Ationo, his eyes widened.

'You!' he said in disbelief.

CHAPTER EIGHT

As he spoke, Atai appeared from behind her house. Ationo smiled her sweetest smile. The smile she received in return seemed to be coated with ice. It gave Ationo the shivers. She knew straight away that the horrible old man had told awful stories about her. What was she to do?

'Why are you back so soon?' enquired Atai. Her voice was very cold.

Ationo was caught off guard. She had not anticipated this question and she did not have a quick lie to answer. However, she recovered her wits quite quickly.

'My grandmother changed her plans,' Ationo lied, 'so I decided to get back home as I was missing my cousin Lilai. Please may I spend the night here?'

The old woman was no fool. She knew immediately that Ationo was lying. However, she just said, 'Certainly. I will be glad to have an extra hand to help me and my brother. He is very tired. He has had a very long journey.'

She looked sharply at Ationo as she spoke. Ationo kept her eyes on the ground. Then Atai spoke again. 'You can stay tonight and move on tomorrow.'

Ationo went into the house and put her luggage where she had placed it before. As she was settling down to rest, Atai called her. She asked Ationo to go to the well to fill up three pots of water. Ationo thought of the gifts, but she did not feel like carrying the heavy pots. She knew she would be leaving early, before they used the water. So, instead of filling three pots, she only filled one. Once she had fetched the water, Ationo settled down again to wait for food.

However, Atai was too wise for Ationo. She decided that this nasty child deserved to be taught a few lessons.

Ationo was very surprised when the old woman called her and asked her to prepare their meal. Atai gave Ationo the same instructions she had given Lilai.

'Go to the granary and fetch half of the millet.'

Ationo went to the granary, but she found only a small amount of millet.

'Why should I halve it?' Ationo said to herself. 'Does she think I have time to waste measuring this out? I'm going to use it all. Hunger can strike her and her brother dead after I'm gone. It will be too late for her to know I did it.'

Once Ationo had fetched the millet Atai told her to thresh half of it. The old woman left the compound and wandered into the nearby bushes looking for herbs to give to her brother.

When Ationo realised that Atai was out of sight, she quickly threshed all the millet. When she had finished threshing, she started to grind the millet into flour.

When the old woman returned she was angry.

'You should wait for instructions! I have my own rules in this house, and you must respect them,' she scolded. 'Anyway, grind half of the millet and leave the other half unground.'

Ationo continued grinding as if nothing had happened. After a few minutes Atai came again. 'Where is the unthreshed millet that I asked you to leave?' she asked.

'Isn't it out there?' asked Ationo. 'Maybe your chickens have feasted on it. I left it there.'

Ationo ground all the millet then she made a fire. She put water on the fire to make millet bread. Then she went to find Atai, and asked her, 'What are we eating with the millet bread?'

The old woman directed her to the pot where she kept dried smoked fish. She told Ationo to get half of the fish to cook. She also added that Ationo should use half of the flour to make millet bread. Ationo ignored the instructions. She cooked all of the fish from the pot. She also used all of the flour she had ground.

When the food was cooked, Atai told Ationo to serve half and to leave half. Again Ationo ignored the instructions. She served all the food.

The three of them had dinner in silence and soon retired to bed. Before Atai fell asleep, she decided that she would give Ationo a present.

The next day, Ationo rose early. She was very excited. She had seen the suitcase in the hut the previous night, and she wondered what colour her jewels would be.

'I have to go home,' she told Atai when she got up. 'My family will be missing me, and I am missing them terribly.'

Atai smiled. 'Well, dear, off you go then,' she said, but she did not offer Ationo anything.

Ationo's high spirits suddenly fell. She could not believe she had wasted her time trying to be good with no reward at all. She turned and walked slowly away, clutching her bundle. But, at the last minute, the old woman called her back. She walked into her hut and came out with the suitcase. Ationo was excited again. Her eyes lit up with a greedy light and she almost forgot to say goodbye in her hurry to get away.

Ationo's instructions were nearly the same as Lilai's. Atai made no mention of returning the suitcase, but she did tell Ationo not to open the suitcase at any cost until she got home. For once, Ationo obeyed. She felt sure that the old woman was a witch, and that her gifts would disappear if she opened the case. However, she was dying to see what was inside, so she ran most of the way home. Carefully, though, in case she tripped and fell and the case opened.

Her eyes lit up with a greedy light.

CHAPTER NINE

The family were very surprised to see Ationo back so soon. Lilai was the first to notice her.

'What are you doing here? Who is looking after Grandmother's place?' she asked in a worried voice.

'Mind your own business!' said Ationo rudely.

Aunt Asio just stared at her daughter, but Ationo's father had reached his limit. He was tired of his daughter's lying and rudeness.

'Come here, you wicked child,' he ordered loudly.

Ationo was shocked. Her father had never spoken to her like this. She slowly walked towards him.

'How is your grandmother?' he asked sternly.

'She is fine,' stammered Ationo. 'But she decided not to go away after all.'

Both parents looked at each other. They knew Ationo well, and they knew she was lying to them.

'Put down that suitcase!' ordered her father. 'And tell us the truth.'

Ationo realised that she was still clutching her precious case. All she wanted was to go inside and see her jewels and clothes. But she knew her parents were very angry. Slowly, she put down the case.

'Well?' asked her father. 'Are you going to tell us the truth or not?'

Ationo said nothing. She stood in front of her parents like a naughty school child. There was a long silence as Ationo just stared at her feet.

Suddenly she realised that her parents were no longer looking at her. She looked in the direction of their stares. They were looking at the suitcase which was moving by itself. It looked like it was dancing or that there was something large inside it trying to get out.

'What sort of pet have you brought back for us?' asked Aunt Asio.

Ationo just stared at the case in horror. It was clear that there was something alive inside it. She was desperately scared. What had that horrible old woman and her brother done?

'Open the case and let us see what you have brought,' demanded her father.

'I . . . No . . . ehm!' stuttered Ationo.

'I said open it!' her father said loudly.

Ationo realised that she had no choice. She walked slowly towards the dancing suitcase. She

She walked slowly towards the dancing suitcase.

could not imagine what was inside to make it dance like that. Cautiously she touched the case. As she touched it, it grew very still. Ationo had never felt so scared in her life.

She knelt down by the case and slowly undid the string. All eyes were on her and the dancing suitcase. Ationo opened the lid and looked inside.

'Aaaieee! Aaaieee!' she screamed and slammed the lid shut quickly. The suitcase was filled with large writhing snakes.

The others had seen inside the suitcase too and were struck dumb with shock. Then Aunt Asio started screaming, 'Snakes! Snakes!' She ran outside, still screaming, followed by Lilai.

Ationo's father tried to be brave, but he too was terrified of snakes and dragged her outside after the others. The suitcase continued to dance towards Ationo, who started to scream again.

Everybody was screaming and shouting. Aunt Asio yelled, 'What have you done? What have you brought back with you? It's bewitched!'

The noise attracted other villagers who came to stare at the spectacle. Everybody soon knew that Ationo had done something bad and brought a curse to the village.

'Take the case back to the old woman!' some people yelled. 'She must be a witch!'

Other people shouted, 'Yes, take it back to the witch and ask for her forgiveness!'

Everybody agreed this was the best thing to do.

Ationo's father said to her, 'You have brought this on yourself. The only way you can undo what you've done is to take the suitcase back to the old woman and tell her you're sorry.'

Ationo, sobbing with fear, was forced to pick up the suitcase. She set off to Atai's house, her feet stumbling on the path. The shouts of her family and the neighbours grew faint behind her.

Nobody really knows what happened to Ationo. Some say that she never found the old woman's hut, that it had disappeared from the face of the earth. Ationo was doomed to be forever tied to the suitcase – every time she put it down, it would dance towards her. If she ran away in one direction, the suitcase would always arrive before her.

Other people say that she did find the old woman, who turned her into a snake for her nasty, selfish ways.

Whatever happened, to this day people in the village of Kareu tell stories of a young girl. Not the one whose beauty turns heads as she passes, but one who walks around carrying a battered old suitcase. She never puts it down, and she is always anxious to help strangers. The villagers warn visitors to stay away from her. Above all, they say, never offer to carry her burden.

Who would want to become the new owner of the dancing suitcase?

Questions

1 Why did Lilai live with her aunt's family?

2 What fears did Lilai have about her journey to her grandmother's home?

3 How did Lilai help the old woman she met along the way?

4 What did Lilai do when she reached her grandmother's house?

5 Why was Lilai's journey home more difficult?

6 What conditions did the old woman attach to Lilai's gift?

7 Why did Ationo want to go and help her grandmother?

8 How did Ationo treat the old man she met on her journey?

9 Why did Ationo leave her grandmother's place so quickly?

10 What happened when Ationo returned home with the suitcase?

11 What do you think happened to Ationo?

Activities

1 Draw Lilai and Ationo. Around each girl write down some words which you think describe their personalities.

2 Imagine that you are Ationo. Make up a story which you would tell to strangers to try and get them to accept the dancing suitcase.

Glossary

affection (page 1) loving fondness

anticipated (page 44) expected

clutching (page 50) holding tightly

cruel (page 36) unkind, nasty

diminishing (page 34) getting smaller

dismay (page 5) worry or concern

distributing (page 22) giving out

dozed (page 17) slept lightly

frail (page 14) weak and unhealthy

glared (page 29) looked angrily

half-heartedly (page 22) without much enthusiasm or involvement

neglected (page 42) badly cared for

papyrus (page 23) reeds which grow near water, used to make mats etc

reluctant (page 6) unwilling, not wanting to

retorted (page 32) replied sharply

rival (page 1) a person who is competing with you

stammered (page 50) spoke unclearly with many pauses

steadfastly (page 5) firmly, not moving

taunted (page 43) teased in an unkind way

tottering (page 34) walking unsteadily, shakily

trivial (page 23) unimportant

wade (page 12) walk slowly through water

writhing (page 53) twisting and rolling

The Junior African Writers Series is designed to provide interesting and varied African stories both for pleasure and for study. There are five graded levels in the series.

Level 3 is for readers who have been studying English for five to six years. The content and language have been carefully controlled to increase fluency in reading.

Content The plots are linear in development, and only the characters and information central to the storyline are introduced. Chapters divide the stories into focused episodes and the illustrations help the reader to picture the scenes.

Language Reading is a learning experience and, although the choice of words is carefully controlled, new words, important to the story, are also introduced. These are contextualised and explained in the glossary.

Glossary Difficult words which learners may not know have been listed alphabetically at the back of the book. The definitions refer to the way the word is used in the story, and the page reference is for the word's first use.

Questions and **Activities** The questions give useful comprehension practice and ensure that the reader has followed and understood the story. The activities develop themes and ideas introduced, and can be done as pairwork or groupwork in class, or as homework.

JAWS Starters
In addition to the five levels of JAWS titles, there are three levels of JAWS Starters. These are full-colour picture books designed to lead in to the first level of JAWS.